My Personal Battle With Covid

Elvina L. Parker

ISBN: 979-8-9865280-8-3 (Paperback edition)
ISBN: 979-8-9889305-0-1 (eBook edition)

Printed in the United States of America
For information about this title or to order books and/or electronic media, contact the publisher:
Sula Too Publishing
www.sulatoo.com/publishing

A Sula Too Tiny Book

"Tiny Books are small enough to fit in your pocket, and big enough to change your life." Sula Too Publishing's Tiny Books feature stories of individuals and organizations that share their formative and celebratory moments, providing inspiration to readers. While each book has a distinct look and feel, they all offer a personal and professional glimpse into the lives of their honorees. They answer important questions about what, when, and most importantly, why these stories are so precious.

Tiny Books offer a sense of comfort to those who relate to their stories and provide valuable insights to those who may not be familiar with the subject matter. The goal of the Tiny Book is to allow the subjects to share important information and memories that they hold dear, and that they feel are significant to their lives.

The Tiny Books can serve as a steppingstone for honorees to write a more comprehensive biography or an autobiography, where they can elaborate on the rest of their story. As a reader, the Tiny Book can also encourage you to share your own story, which is an essential part of our collective history.

This narrative applies to you as reader as well. Your story also needs to be told and now is the time. Your story is our history.

Contents

Dedication

This book is dedicated to my grandson, Rashimir Jumani Burns, and my husband Curtis Parker, Sr.

Acknowledgement

A special thanks to:
Husband, Curtis Parker, Sr.
Pastor Darrell Gilyard, Sr.
Minister Shawn Lax, PA
Cornelius G. Tillman
Salonyia Fisher
Primary Care Physician, Dr. Floyd Willis

Preface

This book is intended to take its place in history and the future.

As a part of history, it documents my experience as one person among so many who lived and some who died.

I leave it to the future to determine how it fits in the grand scheme of things. The future will reveal what is to be learned from all our experiences, including mine.

It Began

I am Elvina L. Parker, and I was diagnosed with COVID in June 2020. Prior to contracting the virus, I had visited one of my primary doctors who had noted that my oxygen levels were dangerously low during a routine checkup. However, she did not take any action and continued with the examination. As my condition worsened, I confided in my girlfriends, Carla A. and Audrey M. expressing that I felt extremely weak and was experiencing coughing spells. Although I had a cough, I didn't initially think much of it. Despite spending most of our days outside by the pool with my grandson during the summer, there were days when I could not join him due to my deteriorating health.

My friend Carla advised me to call Dr. Willis and see about getting a Covid test. I told her I didn't think it was Covid because I clean and wipe everything I touch. I clean with Lysol and or Clorox wipes. But I decided to take her advice and make an appointment to take the test. It was arranged by Dr. Willis for that Friday.

Finally, on June 27, as my condition continued to worsen, I told my husband that I needed to go to the emergency room. I said I'm not getting any better, I was so weak, I couldn't walk by myself down the stairs.

Upon realizing the severity of my condition, my husband and I quickly got dressed and headed to the emergency room. Given the choice between St. Vincent Hospital and Mayo Clinic, I insisted on going to Mayo Clinic.

Upon arrival, they took my vitals and admitted me because my oxygen levels were so low and inquired about whether I had taken a COVID test. I said, I had taken a test few days prior to being hospitalized but had not received my results. My husband was still in the parking lot, during that time no one except the patient was allowed in the hospital. I called my husband and said I'm being admitted for low oxygen levels.

In the hospital emergency room, I was immediately put on oxygen. A specialist in oxygen administration was brought in to regulate the amount of oxygen I received, based on my body weight and needs.

The next day, while still in the hospital, I received the unfortunate news that I had tested positive for COVID-19. I immediately informed my husband and urged him to get tested along with my grandson, Jumani. The doctor began the necessary protocols to manage the situation.

As part of the treatment, I was given a device to measure my lung capacity and expand my lungs. My nurse, Dennis, advised me that the better I performed with the device (incentive spirometer) the better my chances of recovery. He also explained that the device would be my companion throughout my stay. I diligently followed his advice.

I had been hospitalized since the early hours of Sunday morning leading up to this point. I came to the emergency room with a medical history of hypertension, hyperlipidemia, asthma, and low oxygen levels. I was placed on nasal cannula oxygen with continuous oximetry.

The next day I was told I tested positive with COVID. I asked how was that possible? I did everything according to the CDC guidelines. I said when going to the store, if someone came within that 6ft circle, I would say, "Don't you see the sign get back!" I coughed for 3 days, carried a low-grade fever, and was found to have COVID pneumonia.

The doctors came into my room and talked to me about a new drug for covid-19. They indicated if it didn't work, they would put me on the ventilator. I told them to let that be the last resort. At that point, I had to sign off on the new drug. I was treated with Remdesivir, dexamethasone, and Tocilizumab and transferred to the 7th floor. I was then put on a therapeutic for COVID induced pro-coagulopathy.

It Got Serious

Late Thursday night, actually early Friday morning, my husband received a call at 3 a.m. informing him that I had passed out and was found lying on the hospital floor.

First thing I remember was seeing a group of doctors shining lights in my eyes and repeatedly calling my name. "Mrs. Parker, Mrs. Parker can you hear us?" I couldn't respond, and I remember feeling annoyed at their constant chatter and wishing they would be quiet. Little did I know, they were trying to revive me.

According to my husband and the reports, I flatlined twice during this episode. The medical staff asked him if he wanted them to continue resuscitating me, to which he replied in the affirmative, urging them to keep trying until it was no longer possible.

My condition had deteriorated significantly, and the medical staff informed my husband that I only had a 20% chance of surviving. I was about gone! However, I managed to make a partial recovery and regained the ability to speak.

Isolation

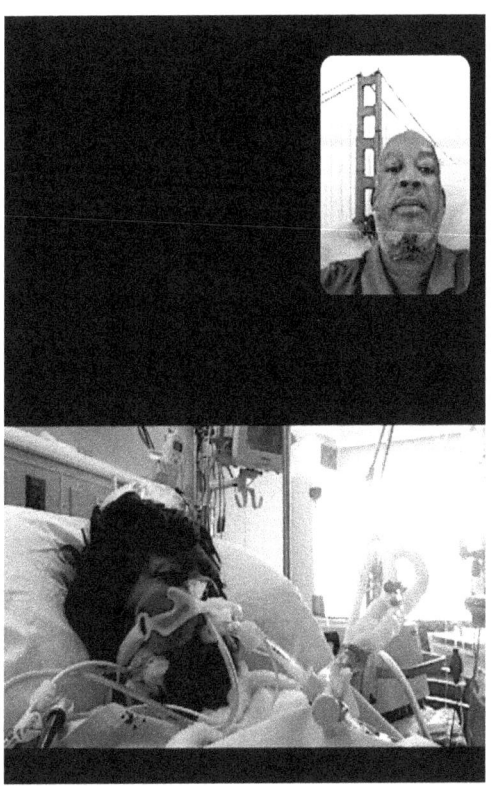

Curtis & Elvina Parker

My husband got upset and had to raise hell somewhat, which was out of character for him. He wanted to see me and couldn't, due to COVID restrictions. My primary doctor at Mayo Clinic invited my husband to a zoom call to discuss my condition.

Visitation restrictions meant that none of my friends and family members were allowed to visit me. To keep my loved ones up to date on my progress, my primary doctor arranged for a daily zoom call at 1 o'clock. The call included my husband, two children, Gerard and Salonyia, Pastor Gilyard, and Minster Shawn Lax, sometimes his wife Veronica, along with the doctors.

For about two weeks, they checked in on me daily to discuss my progress and address any concerns or questions of the medical team. Before getting on the call the nurses would try and make me look somewhat presentable, lipstick, and some mascara. Otherwise, I looked like a hot mess. Even though there were days when I didn't feel like participating on the call, I did my best to smile and communicate as much as possible, despite my inability to talk.

At the end of each zoom call, after the doctors gave their report and answered questions, they exited the zoom call. Before hanging up Pastor Gilyard held a daily prayer with the family and me for the concerns for that day. He concentrated on that specific daily issue. When the doctors were concerned about my hemoglobin, dialysis and kidneys, etc., that is what he prayed about. Everyone was praying for a Miraculous Miracle!

When I could say something, the only person who could understand me was my daughter (Salonyia). I recall my Pastor expressing surprise at how she could decipher my words. Being a mother of three young children, she was accustomed to interpreting unclear speech. Often, I was weak and could only communicate by smiling and waving my hand.

The Treatment

Four days later, I developed progressive worsening hypoxemic respiratory failure due to COVID pneumonia. I developed a large retroperitoneal bleed with increased intra-abdominal pressure, secondary to therapeutic anticoagulation. The bleed was coming from my lower back and a procedure was performed through the groin to stop the bleeding. Coils were placed in the lower back which caused damage to the nerve in the right-side leg, causing a floppy foot.

IR (interventional radiology) performed two abdominal drains.

They were unable to perform an embolization as I developed respiratory failure requiring a code blue for resuscitation paralytics and inotropes. I was transferred to the ICU unit where I required endotracheal intubation. I also had anemia with a hemoglobin of 8.3 which is stable status post blood transfusions and the large retroperitoneal hemorrhage. I developed a larger retroperitoneal hematoma on therapeutic Lovenox for the severe COVID infection. Developed decreased urine output and underwent dialysis catheter placement for initiation of CRRT (Continuous Renal Replacement Therapy). I had persistent abdominal tenderness.

Another World

The doctors and my husband discussed my condition and deterioration concerns. My husband stated he understood my condition and what POC (Point of Care) meant. My husband remained consistent with full and aggressive treatment. The doctors stated he was guarded, not wanting to discuss in detail any overall information about "my poor" prognosis.

My husband told the doctors he was trusting God for a miracle, and that he had to run errands, and it was not the best time to have a conversation. This was the second week of being in the hospital. Otolaryngologists wanted to do a tracheotomy on that Thursday. My husband agreed to have a follow-up after the weekend and would have a discussion with the doctor on Monday.

This required interventional procedure. A surgical procedure in which an incision is made in the front of the neck and a breathing tube is placed into the trachea, also called the windpipe. I was in hemorrhagic shock and developed renal failure requiring CRRT (continuous renal replacement therapy) which had been changed to intermittent hemodialysis. I had persistent leukocytosis and had previously been on Zosyn,

Vancomycin, and Caspofungin. My blood culture was ½ positive for Staph. The following two blood cultures were negative, consistent with what is common in skin. I had respiratory alkalosis.

I was COVID positive on July 6th, 13th, and July 15. I was febrile on multiple readings. I was in hemorrhagic shock and had a mild elevated blood pressure. This was on top of a history of intensive care status to PCU (Progressive care unit) status.

On July 9th, 2020, the staff started talking about (EOL) wishes and at that time my husband wanted to continue aggressive treatment. EOL means, end of life! He wanted to remain Full Code. Hospice was not discussed.

Thanks for having the Palliative Medicine team participate in my care. Sixty-five minutes were spent with greater than fifty percent of the time spent on counseling and coordination of care. This included diagnostic results, impressions, and/or recommended diagnostics studies, risks and benefits of physicians or providers. It also included reviewing information with other physicians to accommodate my needs.

I was in a medically induced coma and on a ventilator for nine days. For the first few days, I was not aware that I was on a ventilator and experienced vivid hallucinations about life, personal and family matters, causing me to undergo a mental transformation. When I was hallucinating, all kinds of things were going through my mind. I didn't really know what was going on.

Since I was unable to speak, I couldn't tell anyone what was in my mind. I believed I had been kidnapped from the Mayo Clinic. In my mind, I had been taken back to my home and handcuffed to my bed.

My husband was there initially, but he left and never came back, which reinforced my belief that I had been kidnapped.

My husband suggested calling JSO and the FBI to get me back, but it was all in my mind. I was going through a delusional phrase, believing that a doctor from the Mayo Clinic had kidnaped me to a house I didn't own. My husband hired a lawyer to sue for my supposed kidnapping from their facility. However, none of it was real. I was actually still in the hospital.

Of course, all of this was a product of my imagination. When I could tell my husband about my "kidnapping," he was understandably confused. My surroundings looked different to me. It seemed to have changed.

In my mind, it had been three or four years when I returned to our current home and asked my husband for some money. He mentioned that he had remarried, but I didn't inquire about his new wife. I assured him that I wasn't trying to ruin his marriage but that I needed help starting over after being gone without a trace.

He provided me with enough money to purchase a condo and a vehicle, and I was grateful for that. However, I couldn't help but wonder if he was still legally married to me while being married to someone else. Despite these thoughts, I didn't try to do anything about it at the time. I thought maybe he's happy. In my mind it only took him a few short years to remarry. During this entire time, I was still on the ventilator and in an induced coma.

One night I crossed my legs and literally could not uncross them. I started to panic a little and pushed my button. I mumbled to the nurse's station I needed help; I couldn't talk clearly because of the damaged vocal cord. Anyway, after a while the nurse got dressed and came to un-cross my legs. Because I had COVID, the entire staff always had to put on a clean gown, gloves, and mask before entering my room.

I didn't understand why I couldn't un-cross my legs, that had never happened before. I had lost a lot of muscle mass. Some have come back, but not all. Even when I came home it hurt to sit on the toilet. It's uncomfortable to walk barefoot on wood or tile floors. The floors were so cold to my feet.

Nine Days

After being in a medically induced coma and on a ventilator for nine days, I overheard the doctors say that they were going to take the *tube* out of me in a couple of days if I was stable. I didn't know I was on a ventilator. I was so grateful they did not mention the word "ventilator". I felt relieved and a sense of peace came over me. It was a peace that surpasses all understanding. I can't explain it, but God!

It never occurred to me I would contract COVID because I was following all the CDC guidelines to keep myself safe. I wore a mask everywhere I went, wiped down everything, and even disinfected my credit or debit cards with hand sanitizer after each use.

During those nine days on the ventilator, when I tell you that God kept me, he truly did. Oh, what peace I had after coming off the ventilator and the induced coma. Because from those dark days until now, I had no worries, because I heard the voice of the Lord say, "Everything Was Going to be Alright." Oh, what peace I had. It was such an unexplainable peace!

I started reciting scriptures in my mind, encouraging myself like David

in the Bible. The scripture says David
encouraged himself.

Proverbs 3:5-6:

Trust in the Lord with all your heart
and lean not on your Own
understanding; In all your ways
acknowledge Him, and He shall direct
your paths.

Psalm: 23

The Lord is my shepherd; I shall not want. He makes me to lie down in green pastures; He leads me beside the still waters. He restores my soul; He leads me in the paths of righteousness For His name's sake. Yea, though I walk through the valley of the shadow of death, I will fear no evil; For You are with me; Your rod and Your staff, they comfort me. You prepare a table before me in the presence of my enemies; You anoint my head with oil; My cup runs over. Surely goodness and mercy shall follow me All the days of my life; And I will dwell in the house of the Lord Forever.

1 John 1-9

If we confess our sins, He is faithful and just to forgive us our sins and to cleanse us from all unrighteousness.

While still in the hospital, I'm not sure if this was after I was off the ventilator and being in a medically induced coma. I remember calling Curtis, but he couldn't really understand me. So, I texted him that if I didn't make it, what to do.

I asked my husband to go into our bedroom and told him which closet to get the outfit I wanted him to bury me in. I told him to hang it on the outside of the closet door. It was an outfit I had purchased a year or so ago and had never worn.

He didn't like me asking him to do such a thing. I just wanted to make sure I was buried in a nice outfit, and I said make sure my lipstick is red.

When I arrived home from rehab, the outfit was still hanging on the closet door.

Philippians 4:13

I can do all things through Christ that strengthens me.

After a few days, the medical team removed the ventilator, but unfortunately, it resulted in damage to one of my vocal cords. Consequently, I was unable to speak at all and had to rely on writing to communicate with the nurses. I was so weak, I could barely hold the pen. I struggled to write legibly and had to undergo extensive speech therapy to strengthen my vocal cords. This process took longer than a couple weeks during the duration of my stay in the hospital. I was told once I leave, the hospital speech therapy would continue during my stay at the rehabilitation center and beyond. It was determined that the right vocal cord was damaged.

Romans 8-28

And we know that all things work together for good to those who love God, to those who are called according to His purpose.

Isaiah 40-31

But those who wait on the Lord Shall renew their strength; They shall mount up with wings like eagles, They shall run and not be weary, They shall walk and not faint.

Psalm 27-1-2

The Lord is my light and my salvation; Whom shall, I fear? The Lord is the strength of my life; of whom shall I be afraid?

Despite being unable to speak, I found comfort in quoting scriptures in my mind. I remembered many verses and began reciting them to myself. In the evenings, before going to bed, I used to listen to music, particularly "Hold on to God's Unchanging Hands," which I began singing to myself. All of this was done way before COVID at night before my prayers and going to bed.

Back To Earth

I began speech therapy, occupational therapy, and physical therapy while still in the hospital. I faced the challenge of having to learn how to walk from scratch. Prior to being put on the ventilator, I was given insulin shots in my stomach area, which resulted in bleeding.

Initially, the source of the bleeding was unknown, but it was eventually traced back to the insulin shots. The bleeding was so severe that I had to undergo a procedure through my groin to stop it and even required a blood transfusion of 15 units. I clearly remember seeing the blood transfusion machine in operation just one day after the incident.

When I regained consciousness, I briefly noticed the blood transfusion machine before drifting off again. Subsequently, my kidneys ceased to function correctly.

Dialysis

On July 11, 2020, dialysis was started. I went through dialysis treatment three times a week for about two weeks while still in the hospital.

Each dialysis session was incredibly draining, and it sapped all my energy. Even before leaving the hospital, my medical team was already considering the best rehabilitation options for my situation. This included arranging for dialysis treatment three times a week.

During the two months that I was hospitalized and in rehab, I was too weak to even comb my hair. When I regained the energy, I would text my husband and ask him to send me some turbans to wear on my head. Occasionally, some kind nurse would apply a little bit of lipstick and mascara to help me look somewhat presentable.

After the blood transfusion, they inserted coils through my groin to stop the bleeding, which is now located in my lower back. Unfortunately, this procedure damaged some nerves on my right side, which has affected my ability to walk and run like I used to. For extended periods of walking, I require a walker, and for shorter distances or around the house, I use a cane. The cane is because of the limp and to keep me from having a "slip and fall" accident.

Prior to COVID, I had an active routine that included 95 to 100 jumping jacks every morning and attending weekly line dancing classes. Also, going to the gym. Each year I participated in the Kappa Alpha Psi 5k Healthy Start run/walk. In January 2020, I won 3rd place in my age group. I also participated in various annual run/walk events throughout the city. Upon leaving the rehab center, I could no longer do these activities.

Rehabilitation

Before they could release me to a rehabilitation center, the doctors were trying to find one that could accommodate my weekly treatments.

The day I was supposed to be discharged from the hospital; I was scheduled for an early morning dialysis treatment. But God intervened and my kidneys no longer needed dialysis treatments. I was carried back to my room and dialysis was no longer needed. God is so good! What a mighty God we serve.

I asked my husband how I was going to be transported from the hospital to

Cypress Village Rehab? He said, "In a rescue vehicle, Elvina." I said, "That's not going to work, it's too close a confinement, I'm claustrophobic, you know that I can't do that! Not an option! You need to find another way." When he had no words to satisfy me, he said, "Elvina." I said, "Curtis, I might jump out the rescue."

That day, I was in anticipation mode needless to say all day! I didn't know what to expect for my 5-mile ride to my new rehab center for the next 30 or so days before going home.

EMT was about two hours late picking me up. However, the EMT staff members very professional, and they were in a larger rescue vehicle than those I see on a daily basis.

Curtis met the EMT at Cypress Village Rehab and the EMT's allowed us to hug and talk to each other before carrying me into the facility. Curtis was still not able to visit any health care facilities. I settled in ok, with the rehab facilities, but was not given any dinner the first night. It was past dinner time, so I got snacks.

Before starting speech therapy at the rehab my speech was like a whisper, Curtis understood some just really weak. I mostly, smiled. With receiving daily speech therapy, my voice gradually returned. It was very weak, but over time it became better I was given extensive speech therapy.

Before leaving the rehab center, I was allowed to take showers three times a week. The first time, it felt like the best I had taken in my life. Since I couldn't stand up alone, I had to sit while washing, always assisted by the nurse technician because I couldn't wash my back etc.

When I washed my feet, nothing but dirt that was washing off my body and especially my feet. It had been almost two months since I've had a good full bath or shower. While in the hospital and rehab center, I was given sponge baths twice daily.

With receiving daily speech therapy, my voice gradually returned. It was initially weak, but it grew stronger.

I spent 33 days in rehab.

I started reciting scriptures in my mind, encouraging myself to think positive thoughts and not fill my mind with negative thoughts.

Most people say that my voice sounds the same as it did before. Earlier, I forgot to mention that I have asthma, which is another underlying condition.

At the time, I didn't realize that it was also a factor in my COVID-19 experience.

That was the reason why I was coughing so much. I had an inhaler, but I didn't use it as frequently as I should. I only used it during pollen season and winter months, but not as much during the summer months.

This happened in June 2020 when I turned 65. I was also planning on changing my name to Emerald. Even though my attorney friend had sent the legal papers to me, I was too sick complete them and some people call me Emerald.

I bought a bicycle for myself to keep exercising, but only rode it once before getting COVID. I'm working on being able to line dance, despite the nerve damage, which has now resulted in neuropathy.

My physical therapist, Robert, was also a nice Christian young man. During my weekly visits with him, we would often talk about the goodness of the Lord.

Male phlebotomist can in my room exactly, 4:00 am each morning while I was in the hospital. He never smiled, never spoke, or asked me which arm was good for getting blood. He knew I had small veins. I was so glad when he was moved to another floor, I didn't get know what to do!

Everyone else would come between 5:00 - 5:30 am. My arms were black and blue by the time I left both the hospital and rehab. Once I was home, I mentioned to Carla, she brought me some vitamin E oil.

After being discharged from rehab, I had to revisit all the doctors who had treated me during my COVID illness. They were surprised to see how much my appearance had changed. Looking back, I did resemble my 88-year-old mother at the time.

When I returned home, my husband remarked on how much I looked like my mother, which I found hurtful because I knew I looked much older due to the grueling two-month ordeal. During my illness, I had lost around 40 pounds, and my weight had dropped to a mere 111 pounds. I looked incredibly thin, and my clothes hung off me, making me appear like a skeleton. I was a bag of bones.

However, I was home and surrounded with symbols of love. There was an outpouring of flowers that was lined up at my home from family members, neighbors and friends! It looked like a florist. Give me my flowers while I live so that I can see them.

New Body

My recovery involved a physical therapist, an occupational therapist, a speech therapist, urologist, neurologist, ear nose and throat, and a nurse. Every specialist except a cardiologist, oncologist, and a psychiatrist. Praise the Lord! When it was all said and done, I had a new body.

One day, I realized that I needed to start buying clothes that little people wear, as I had lost a significant amount of weight. Since the only places I was going were doctor's appointments and home for physical and occupational therapy, I asked my husband to take me to the store. We bought a few pairs of leggings and smaller tops so that I could at least dress in clothes that fit the size I really was.

After leaving rehab, my appointments started with the neurologist every other day. Various painful tests were given to determine the extent of the damage to my nerves. The pain was excruciating, but it was necessary to get a proper diagnosis. The tests revealed that the nerves on the right side of my body had been damaged and needed time to regenerate.

The neurologist informed me in November 2020, that it would take three to six months for the nerves to regrow as they could only grow certain centimeters at a time.

During the three-to-six-month period, I was able to feel the nerves in my feet when it was some activity going on. It was very weird and uncomfortable feeling.

However, as of June 2021, there had not been a significant change, even after taking a second nerve test. The doctor said, "While there are no guarantees," I'm still praying and depending on the Lord to get back 100%.

Currently, I'm reading a book called, *Demand Your Healing* and putting my faith in the promises of God throughout this entire ordeal! Mr. & Mrs. Womack gave me this book while I was still in rehab.

Once I got home, I couldn't use the regular bathtub and had to have a nurse help me take a bath.

Throughout this journey, I had no privacy! My husband ordered a walk-in tub to accommodate my needs, but it didn't arrive in time, I had to wait until September 10, 2020, before it was installed. By this time, I had returned home from rehab at the end of August 2020.

Eight or nine months following the nerve test in November 2020, the neurologist said that my nerves on the right side needed to grow back and that it could take three to six months for the nerve to grow a certain number of centimeters.

The nurse came to help me with my bath three times a week, along with my occupational therapist and physical therapist who also came three times a week.

I particularly enjoyed my occupational therapist as she worked on my upper body. She always recommended different equipment for strength training. I told Curtis and he ordered whatever was needed. She enjoyed our appointments and loved that we lived in the same neighborhood as her parents.

My physical therapist was also a nice Christian guy. After about a month, I didn't need the nurse to assist me with my bath anymore.

Curtis was able to help me get into the walk-in spa bathtub that was installed I could sit down and give myself a bath. He would help me get out when it was time, and then I would sit down again and dry myself off before getting dressed for bed.

I continued with my at-home physical therapist until May 2021, when I was discharged around Mother's Day. It was suggested that I join a gym and hire a personal trainer, which I did, and I now go two to three times a week.

However, I still need more physical therapy to help me get stronger and prevent falls, so I plan to start in-house physical therapy soon. Although I only use my cane 10% of the time, I still have to be cautious not to trip or fall.

Mobilization

My husband always accompanied me to all my appointments and wheeling me in my wheelchair. I think he enjoyed pushing my chair, even carrying me whenever necessary. But I didn't like the idea of relying on him all the time, I didn't have a choice, especially for shopping.

The day after leaving rehab, I had a hair appointment scheduled, and my husband drove me there. I suggested that he could leave me there and come back to pick me up later, which he did a few times. I would typically get my hair done every two to three weeks, depending on how it looked.

I informed my physical therapist, Robert, that I needed to learn how to operate my car using my right foot. That foot had been giving me the most trouble. Robert promised that during his next visit, he would take me on a drive around my neighborhood to help me practice.

However, before he could return, I had made other plans. I told Curtis I wanted to drive my car around the neighborhood, he said I'm going with you to ensure my safety. After backing out the garage, I talked to my foot and urged it to work for me, and it did. I was so happy, and I knew it was mind over matter.

One day, I needed to go to my pharmacist at CVS, so I decided to drive myself. My husband offered to go with me, I said, "If you like that would be nice."

After that, I realized I could drive myself wherever I wanted to go. At first, I only drove short distances. Within three months, I was able to drive to the shopping mall. I felt really good about that. However, the nerve in my right foot still has not fully recovered, and I still experience pain in my legs and feet at night.

It takes me two to three hours to fall asleep at night because I'm constantly rubbing and feeling my legs and feet, which can feel cold, stinging or burning. It is definitely painful. I have regular leg cramps at night in both legs, hurt so bad.

My second physical therapist gave me a set of exercises to help with my foot movement.

I experience a burning sensation every night, especially in my right foot, which has been the most problematic. Before going to bed, I apply a cream to help me endure the discomfort caused by the nerves, or whatever is going on in my legs. I have to elevate my legs in bed every night to prevent blood clots and keep the circulation flowing. I also massage my legs to alleviate the burning sensation.

Additionally, I am careful when getting up, and I make sure to watch my movements to prevent any accidents. I do this each time I attempt to get up, it's crucial for my safety.

I use a foot spa once or twice a week with Epsom salt to reduce swelling in my feet. Most times during the day I wear compression socks and before going to bed I put on regular socks to keep my feet warm. Before Covid, I wouldn't have thought of wearing socks to bed was unthinkable.

I often hear people say, "I don't feel well", and sometimes it seems to be the last thing they say before expressing that they are really sick. I experienced this myself, feeling weak every day leading up to my hospitalization. I believed my protein levels were low and often during the day I would often eat almonds or peanut butter, which seemed to make me feel better.

However, I didn't realize that my weakness was actually due to my oxygen levels decreasing, which was caused by my asthma. I also experienced excessive coughing, which I now know I should have been treated with my inhaler. These were the symptoms I was experiencing.

Unlike most people who lost their sense of smell, I never experienced this symptom. However, I did lose my sense of taste which is one reason why I lost a significant amount of weight during my hospital stay. I found it difficult to enjoy the food I was given and often only ate small portions. At Cypress Village, they served us three meals a day at 8am, 12pm, and 5pm, which I found to be too early for breakfast. I would often look at my food and struggle to eat it.

Each day, my husband would ask how I enjoyed my food. I would say it was ok. However, I didn't eat all of it because I didn't have a taste for food. In fact, I often just held it in my mouth. Gross, but I did. Yuck!

He was in constant contact with my case manager, making sure I was eating something. I will say, he was on top of everything going on with me. During my hospital stay and while in rehab, he made sure the staff knew what I needed and what he wanted to happen.

Don't let me tell my husband something I didn't particularly like or cared for, from staff upsetting me, he would reach out to my case manager, and she would speak to the staff.

The staff noticed my lack of appetite and the person in charge of scheduling patient meals, who I believe was a dietitian, came to my room one day during my rehab stay. She asked me about my food preferences and tried to adjust my meal plan accordingly.

However, because my sense of taste was off, none of the food tasted good to me. Despite this, I knew I had to eat something to stay alive, so I tried my best to eat what was given to me. It was like the saying "eating to live instead of living to eat." I wanted test results to be positive.

After completing my rehab program, I returned home at the end of August. Around September or October my sense of taste began to improve. My husband told my doctor she needed to advise me to gain some weight. However, she said that I looked fine. The doctor told me that I could eat whatever I wanted, so that's what I did. Although I didn't gain back all the weight I had lost before COVID, I feel like I'm at a good weight now.

I used to go outside with my grandson, but I couldn't stay out there for long because I would start feeling unwell and would need to go back to bed. At the time, I didn't realize that my body was lacking in vitamin D, which is essential for good health. Now I understand the importance of vitamin D, take supplements, and spend at least 20 minutes in the sun each day to get the natural vitamin D.

When I turned 65, I decided that I wanted to change my look. On June 10th, the day before my birthday, I went to my hairstylist and asked for a short haircut. It was a big change for me, as I had never had short hair before. When she finished cutting it, I was initially worried that it would be difficult to manage, but over time it has grown back and is now looking good.

Before COVID, I worked part-time at a school as a substitute teacher and also did aftercare in the afternoons for a Christian school. I continued doing that until March 6, 2020, when everything changed due to the pandemic. Prior to that, I had plans to enroll in a line dancing class. I used to dance once a week with a group before the pandemic. My husband and I are retired, and we had the opportunity to travel to London, Paris, Rome, and Florence.

It's easy to take things for granted, like walking, until you are unable to do it like you used to. I have always enjoyed walking around our neighborhood and nearby park.

I have received both doses of the COVID-19 vaccine and three boosters. This book is to encourage as many people as possible to get the vaccination and continue getting the yearly boosters. Most importantly, the Miracles and Blessings of God! Without God, I know I wouldn't have made it! I thank God every day!

When I was asked about my opinion on the vaccine prior to its availability, I expressed I wished it had been available when I contracted COVID-19. I have no issues with taking the vaccine and I am not hesitant about it like some people who may have concerns about its safety. I received the Pfizer shot and did not experience any aftereffects. Given my health scare last year and the low survival odds given by doctors, I am grateful that I was able to take the vaccine.

Yes, I was glad that I took it, especially with what I went through last year. When the doctors give your family and friends your chance of survival, you will do whatever is necessary.

Prayer First

My husband called for the prayer warriors to pray the word of prayer from many believers of the word of God. It's important to know how to pray and can get a prayer through.

Curtis asked who we should contact first, I said Mrs. Raye, the Pastor, my children (Gerard, Salonyia), Willa, a few friends, and church members. I needed people that knew how to really pray and get a prayer through to God.

My mother and my siblings were told a few days later that I had been hospitalized. We wanted to know if it warrants telling others until we realized the severity of my condition. My mother was 88 years old, and we didn't want to cause her blood pressure to skyrocket.

Covid Fear

The pandemic brought many changes to how we live our lives as uncertainty, altered daily routines and social isolation. We had concerns about getting sick and how long the pandemic would last. It is normal to feel afraid even now but pay attention to if it starts to turn into panic.

While fear, anxiety, and panic can all look similar, fear is a more immediate response to a direct threat. We all have mixed emotions about everything.

2 Timothy 1-7: For God has not given us the spirit of fear, but of power and of love and of a sound mind. One of

the best things for me to get closer to God while battling Covid-19. God cares for me, and knows what I need before I ask, and he understands my heart.

Worrying about Covid or anything else only increased depression and mental problems. I chose to rejoice in the Lord and his goodness and mercy.

Philippians 4, 6, 7: "Be anxious for nothing, but in everything by prayer and supplication, with Thanksgiving let your request be known to God; and the peace of God, which surpasses all understanding, will guard your hearts and minds through Christ Jesus."

The day after being discharged from the rehab, I had a salon appointment to have my hair done. My husband carried me to my appointment, and I was greeted by Audrey, one of my girlfriends, that greeted me with open arms and hugs. She was glad to see me.

My husband said, "You can't hug her, she's just getting out of rehab." He knew that I had a negative covid test and that I hadn't been around other people in a while. He cautioned her about physical contact due to my recent illness, but I was touched by her warm gesture. Despite this, I found it interesting that my friends were eager to embrace me, yet my own mother remained hesitant to hug me.

I have not denied the fact that many people did not survive the illness I went through. However, I consider it a miracle of God and a blessing that I am still here today.

During my illness, I had a conversation with the Lord in my mind and he assured me that everything would be alright. I told him that I had lived a good life and if it was my time to go, I was ready.

There were two places I wanted to visit before leaving this world: Australia and Bora Bora. Although our plans to visit Australia had to be canceled due to the pandemic, I still held onto the hope of traveling there one day. As I talked to the Lord, I mentioned the Bible's promise of a prepared place for believers and said that if it was my time to leave, I was ready to go to heaven. The streets will be paved with gold, and I would have a mansion there.

However, the Lord saw fit to keep me alive, so I can share his goodness and mercy and for that, I'm grateful.

I have written this very personal information because I wanted to share my experience and the importance of my faith in the Lord in overcoming my illness. It's important for people to know how I was able to get through it. When I returned home, my friend Carla was so delighted that God had healed me from this deadly disease.

When I returned home, someone called me and said, "you did it, girl." At first, I considered leaving it at that, but I said, "God did it." I wanted to give God all the Glory, and not me! My friend prayed for me while I was hospitalized and cried often for her friend. I will forever be thankful and grateful! God is so good, and his promises are true.

Hebrews 11:1 Now faith is the substance of things hoped for, the evidence of things not seen.

I have always had unwavering faith in God, especially after what he did for me. I am confident that God will always be there for me, and I will forever give him thanks and praise.

The power of prayer is amazing, as shared by my friend Willa Peterson:

June 2022, and even now is a time when we all are witnessing God prove Himself faithful in this Scripture verse and so many more. I called my beloved friend, Elvina, on June 11, 2020, to wish her a happy birthday. About ten days later, I received a text from Elvina asking me to pray for her because she had been diagnosed with COVID19. I did only what I knew to do and that was to round up the prayer warriors and PRAY! I began with our dear friends, Irma Daniels, and Diane Reid, who has since transitioned to be with the Lord. We knew and held on to Deuteronomy 32:30, The prayers of one will send a thousand to flight and the prayers of two to ten thousand. So, we went into a serious battle through prayer and claimed the victory before it manifested. Oh, but we didn't stop there. We each contacted our other prayer groups and friends and had them interceding in prayer for Elvina and Curtis.

Although we prayed, Satan was relentless. We received almost daily reports from Elvina's faithful husband, Curtis, who kept us updated on Elvina's progress. Some reports were bleak, from Elvina having to have a tube in her stomach, to kidney failure and the need to be on dialysis. However, we were determined to "Walk by faith and not by sight." 2 Corinthians. 5:7"

We were trusting and standing on unwavering faith that God would do what His Word declared was already done: by His stripes Elvina was already healed. 1 Peter 2:24

We knew the one thing Satan could not stand was our praise! With each update we received from Curtis whether challenging or victorious, we gave a pre-praise for the challenging reports and a Hallelujah, thank You, Jesus for the reports of victory.

Curtis went into spiritual warfare with another weapon on Satan by sending out daily inspirational messages and Bible verses about God's goodness. Then, around mid-July, we received the praise report! Elvina was able to respond to commands by blinking her eyes and by squeezing the doctor's hand! Prayer was still needed for Elvina to get off the ventilator, successfully breathe on her own, and that the spikes that make up the crown of the virus would dissolve. Prayers were being answered! Near the end of July, Elvina was out of ICU, and on her way to being admitted to physical therapy! The best news came on August 26, 2020, a few days later Elvina was cleared to go home! TO GOD BE THE GLORY FOR THE GOOD THINGS HE HAS DONE!

Friend Willa Peterson

Finding Normal

I am still going through it. Even after leaving the hospital, one of the issues I faced was not being able to urinate, which resulted in me needing a catheter. This continued for over six hours, and even now, with a new urologist, I still have problems. It's draining to deal with ongoing issues after having COVID, especially since there wasn't a clear treatment plan at first. Additionally, there were other health concerns I faced during that time that I may or may not include in the book. I was in the hospital for six or seven days, so that's when some of these issues arose.

The first time my husband and I attempted to have intimacy was around four or five months after being released from the rehab center and after my medical issues began.

It was extremely painful, almost like I was a virgin again. It had to do with the nerves on my right side. After several months, it was still painful, which is unusual. I went to my OB-GYN and explained my situation. She recommended a product to use, and it worked. Praise God!

I think we're going to be dealing with COVID for quite a while and people need to know.

In 2020 and 2021 alone, before the vaccine was available, over 700,000 people lost their lives to COVID-19. By 2023 the total number of deaths in the US surpassed 900,000. It's hard to comprehend the scale of this tragedy, as most of us have lost someone; friends, a distant relative, or close family members. I experienced it firsthand when my oldest sister passed away while I was still in the hospital.

She didn't have COVID, but she had dementia and was in a nursing home.

Then, in November of 2020, I lost two first cousins to COVID-19. One of them went to the hospital for another reason and developed COVIS-19 while there. Sadly, I couldn't attend their funerals.

My grandson is someone very special to me, even though he has Down Syndrome, our bond is unbreakable. He lives in Atlanta with his mother and two sisters, but he loves visiting me. In 2020 when I fell sick, he was so sad and wanted to be with me. When I was in the hospital my grandson was with my husband, every night they would facetime me and at the end of each call, he would ask to pray for me. I welcome his prayers and I truly believe God heard his prayers, and for that I am grateful.

In 2022, I planned a trip to St. Maarten with him, but we realized we had misplaced his passport. Despite expediting it, we received it just two days before our departure date, which meant we couldn't make the trip. Instead, we went to Orlando, and I made sure we had a good time together. He left on that Friday, and I know he missed me, but he had to go back to school.

In the hospital, I remember how much I cried when I received text messages about someone passing away. It was tough being separated from loved ones.

COVID-19 has had a significant impact on our lives, including an increase in psychiatric symptoms like anxiety, insomnia, and depression. Despite this, there are steps we can take to improve our health and well-being, such as adopting a healthier diet and engaging in physical activity regularly.

To achieve the longest and healthiest life possible, I am taking the following steps:

- Engaging in physical activity every day
- Eating a diet rich in whole grains, lean protein, leafy green vegetables, fruits, and nuts

- Ensuring I get enough vitamins and calcium
- Maintaining a healthy weight and body shape
- Exercising my mind and focusing on positive thoughts every day
- Reading God's word on a daily basis
- Building strong bones and body mass
- Drinking more water and staying hydrated
- Getting enough restful sleep
- Avoiding negative influences in my life
- Incorporating a variety of colorful fruits and vegetables into my diet

- Choosing healthy snacks
- Striving for happiness and enjoyment in my life
- Connecting with others and sharing my thoughts and feelings
- Visiting my primary care doctor for yearly check-ups and exams.

COVID -19 survivors, like me, may experience "long-haul" effects such as neurological symptoms and mental conditions. These symptoms may include difficulty concentrating, headaches, sleep problems, dizziness upon standing, pins-and-needles sensations, loss of smell or taste, as well as depression or anxiety.

I have neurological symptoms on the right side of my body and in both legs and feet. For a couple years I was unable to crawl into bed. I had to turn around and push backwards to get in the bed. because crawling into bed hurt my knees.

We take so much for granted, who would have thought getting into bed would be a hindrance! I crawled! Still praying. My cross to bear!

I had to learn how to walk again. My legs and feet are particularly affected at night, with tingling and burning sensations. However, I am grateful to have regained my sense of taste and smell. Praise be to God for that!

Coughing is a natural defense mechanism that helps to protect the lungs by expelling irritants. During recovery from certain infections, including COVID-19, the lungs can become irritated, resulting in a dry cough. The duration of this cough is uncertain and can be frustrating; in some cases, it may persist for years. While a dry cough is a common symptom of COVID-19, some individuals may experience a cough with phlegm. In my case, I have had a dry cough for years, and it still persists two years after my COVID-19 diagnosis.

I visited my ear, nose, and throat (ENT or otolaryngologist) specialist to have a nasal endoscopy to look at the nasal and sinus passages. It's done with an endoscope. It's a thin, flexible tube with a tiny camera and a light. This procedure caused a great deal of discomfort and pressure as the tube was put into my nose. The spray numbs your nose, mouth, and throat. I felt like I couldn't swallow. I also felt discomfort, I started coughing and felt nauseous. The ENT had to stop the procedure.

I also had an appointment with a urologist assistant who recommended some products for me to use at home and when out during social events. She showed me how to sit in a position like a frog. I would not have to sit in the same position in public.

One night, I heard Reverend James Cleveland's "Peace Be Still" and a voice telling me that everything would be alright. It brought me a sense of peace and security. Although there was no one standing guard gave me the peace that I needed to get through what I was going through.

"The Master of ocean and earth and skies, They shall sweetly obey my will. Peace be still, peace be still. They all shall sweetly obey my will, peace be still."

My Testimony

After God miraculously healed me from COVID -19, I received a voice message from a person I know. She stated they were glad when they found out I was in the hospital with COVID, they were so elated and hope I died!

This was about 6 months after getting out of the hospital and rehab. Of course, Satan would have loved nothing more than for me to be despondent by such a cruel message however, I chose to focus and rejoice in the goodness of God.

Till this day I've not responded to the message, it's in God's hand! Although I was gravely ill, God's Word says No weapon formed against me shall prosper. **Isaiah 54:17** COVID – 19 did not prosper over me! God's Word says in **Romans 8:31** What then shall we say to these things? If God is for us, who can be against us?

Because God is for me and is my shield, I know no fiery darts will prevail against me. I rejoice knowing I am more than a conqueror through Him who loved me. God's word triumphs over the power of thoughts, words, and intentions set against me.

1 Cor. 15:57 But thanks be to God, who gives us the victory through our Lord Jesus Christ. I praise God daily for the victory over COVID and every hindering spirit sent by the evil one. To God be the glory for the great things He has done for Me!

Praise God – Life continues……

About the Author

Elvina L. Parker was born in Eustis, Florida on June 11,1955 to Mr. Willie L. Lewis, Sr and Delvernia Lewis. She had 5 sisters (her oldest sister, Odessa, passed while Elvina was hospitalized) and one brother who grew up in Wildwood, Florida.

Upon graduation, she moved to Jacksonville, Florida to attend Massey Business College and Jacksonville University College. She received BS degree in Liberal Arts, a minor in Business Administration, and a minor in Religion from Jacksonville University.

She was employed by Blue Cross and Blue Shield for 19 years; 4-5 years she worked as a paralegal; and ended her career with Duval Schools as a substitute teacher. She currently works parttime for a private Christian school as the front desk receptionist.

Elvina is married to Curtis E. Parker, Sr., have two adult children (Gerard and Salonyia), two stepchildren (Cecily and Curtis, II), and three grandchildren (Rashimir, Susie, and Ciara).

Elvina was a member of the Continental Societies, Inc. for nine years. The Continental Societies, Inc is an International Service Organization dedicated to the socioeconomic and cultural welfare of underserved children and youth.

Elvina is a member Kappa Alpha Psi, Silhouette Chapter Jacksonville, Florida Chapter. As such, they support their husbands in their projects including feeding the hungry.

She is a member of Mt. Ararat Missionary Baptist Church.

She loves shopping and traveling. She is learning to play beginner's Bridge. She considers herself blessed to have traveled to many places and to have crossed several items off of her bucket list.

TO GOD BE THE GLORY!

My Cross to Bear!

www.ingramcontent.com/pod-product-compliance
Lightning Source LLC
Chambersburg PA
CBHW051536120626
46551CB00012B/1255